foulsham
The Publishing House, Bennetts Close, Cippenham,
Slough, Berkshire, SL1 5AP, England

ISBN 0-572-02558-0

Previously published as *Cunning Stunts*

Printed in Great Britain
by St Edmundsbury Press Ltd
Bury St Edmunds, Suffolk.

CONTENTS

Have you ever wished you had a store of tricks to astound your friends, brighten up a flagging conversation or liven up a dull party?
Well, here they are – a collection of simple but effective stunts, challenges and tricks for you to try out on your friends. Plus a few for those who aren't quite so friendly! Some are simplicity itself to perform – you only have to remember the trick.
Others require a little bit of practice but it's well worth it to achieve stunning effects.

Good luck!

THE TABLE CLOTH TRICK

This trick is a variation of the famous 'Pulling a Tablecloth Away Leaving the Crockery on the Table' trick, and I must say that learning this version of the trick has been a godsend for us, we only hope you may benefit by learning this trick as much as we have!

The reason it has helped us so much is, after a few drinks and a lot of loud encouragement from so-called friends, my writing partner and good friend Ian Alexander is prone to attempt the 'real' tablecloth trick... unfortunately, this trick should only be performed stone cold sober, by professionals. The version you are about to learn, we have found, is just as much fun, cheaper, and you don't get thrown out if it goes wrong...

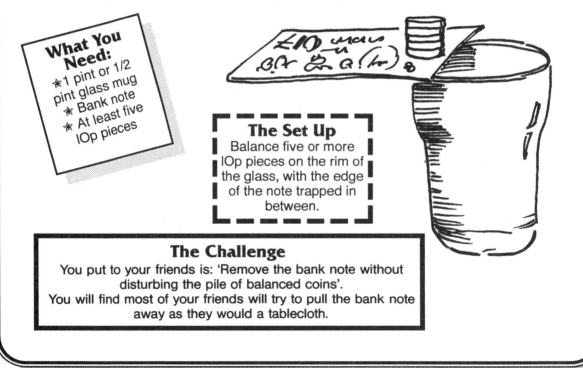

What You Need:
* 1 pint or 1/2 pint glass mug
* Bank note
* At least five 10p pieces

The Set Up
Balance five or more 10p pieces on the rim of the glass, with the edge of the note trapped in between.

The Challenge
You put to your friends is: 'Remove the bank note without disturbing the pile of balanced coins'.
You will find most of your friends will try to pull the bank note away as they would a tablecloth.

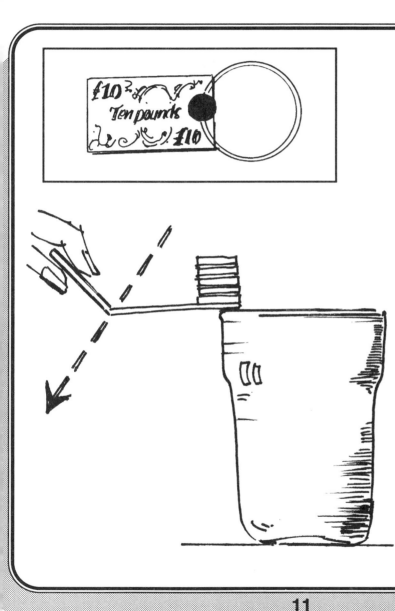

How It's Done

Once the coins and bank note are set up, gently take the free end of the bank note between your thumb and forefinger and gently raise the bank note to create an angle.

While retaining your hold on the bank note, strike down with the forefinger of your other hand in the position and direction shown.

To increase the degree of difficulty, simply add more coins, and/or position the centre of the bank note closer to the coins.

GOOGLY GLASSES

Googly Glasses is a trick I like to perform just before leaving a bar, almost as a calling card. You are bound to be remembered the next time you walk in. It is also a great conversation piece if you just do it and let people discover it for themselves.

The Challenge
To balance the glasses, one on top of the other, on their outer rims.

Your friends will find this impossible because they don't know the '10 o'clock and 2 o'clock secret'.

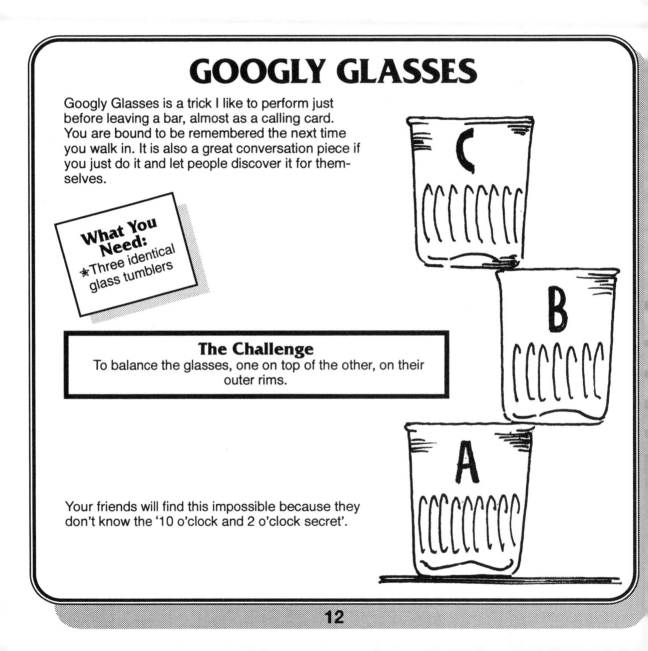

How It's Done

Place bottom glass A on a counter. Looking from above, imagine a clock dial around the top rim.

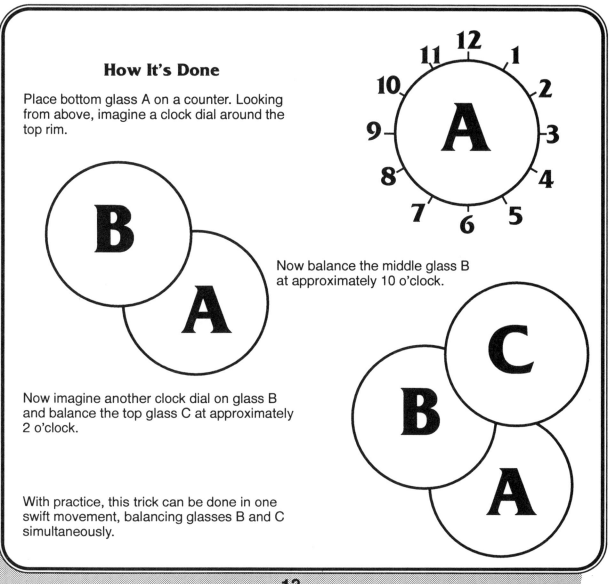

Now balance the middle glass B at approximately 10 o'clock.

Now imagine another clock dial on glass B and balance the top glass C at approximately 2 o'clock.

With practice, this trick can be done in one swift movement, balancing glasses B and C simultaneously.

BRANDY AND SHERRY GLASS CHALLENGE

The Brandy and Sherry Glass Challenge is a great trick to keep in mind if you are going to a party.

One thing to remember with a trick of this nature, whereby the performance is also the secret, make great play of setting the challenge, challenge a lot of people at the same time and you will gain the maximum effect, and fun!

What You Need:
✳ A brandy glass (with a drink in it!)
✳ A sherry glass

The Set Up
Place the brandy glass with the liquid in it on to a table and place the up-turned sherry glass inside the brandy glass.

The Challenge
Drink the brandy from the sherry glass, but you cannot touch the sherry glass with your hands.

How it's Done

1. Pick up the brandy glass in your hand.

2. Bend forward and take the far side of the sherry base in your mouth and remove the sherry glass from the brandy glass.

3. Stand up straight and tip your head back. This now puts the sherry glass the right way up.

4. Pour the liquid from the brandy glass carefully into the sherry glass.

5. Turn the now empty brandy glass upside down and with your mouth, slide the sherry glass onto the brandy glass. You are now holding an up-turned brandy glass with the sherry glass standing on its base.

6. Because of the size of a sherry glass you can now put the whole top end of the sherry glass into your mouth, pick it up, tip your head back and you have taken the drink from the sherry glass without touching it with your hands.

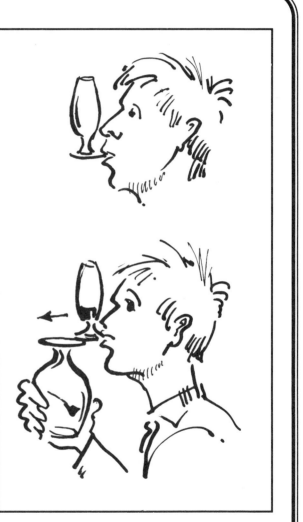

THE SUPER-STICKY PENNY

The Super-sticky Penny is a trick I performed on the BBC's Les Dennis Laughter Show. We filmed this trick by stopping people in the street at random and setting the challenge - and a good time was had by all.

What You Need:
* A penny
* An ashtray or saucer
* A friend with a sense of humour

The Set Up
In this trick you stick a penny on your forehead and gently, repeat GENTLY, tap your chin on the bar until the penny drops into the ashtray.

The Challenge
Your friend has to do the same but when they try they will find it impossible.

How it's Done

The reason you can do it and they can't is a simple one: they only think that there is a coin on their forehead.

First of all, press a penny on to your own forehead for at least 10 seconds. Now gently tap your chin on the bar as you do this - if you frown the penny will immediately fall off and land in the ashtray. Simple!

Now it is your friend's turn. You do not allow your friend to stick the penny on their own forehead. You do it.

As you are pressing the coin on your friend's forehead, have your fingernail under the edge of the coin. After pressing for at least 10 seconds, simply lift the coin up and away without your friend seeing it. Your friend will still 'feel' the coin on their forehead.

Now you watch as your friend tries to dislodge a coin that isn't there, much to the delight of everyone present.

THE FLYING FIFTY

The Flying Fifty is another trick that I performed as part of a feature called 'Martin Daniels' Challenge' on BBC's Les Dennis Laughter Show.

What You Need:
- ✴ One 50p piece
- ✴ 1 pint beer mug (or coffee mug with similar diameter)

The Set Up
Balance the 50p on the rim of the beer mug.

The Challenge
Blow the 50p directly over the diameter of the beer mug without the 50p touching the glass at all!

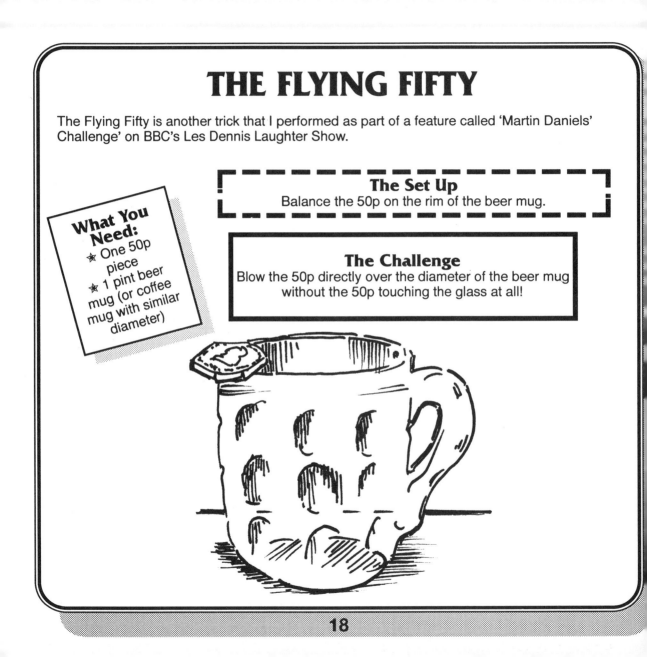

How it's Done

Blow down on the outside of the coin.

This will deflect it up and forward over the glass.

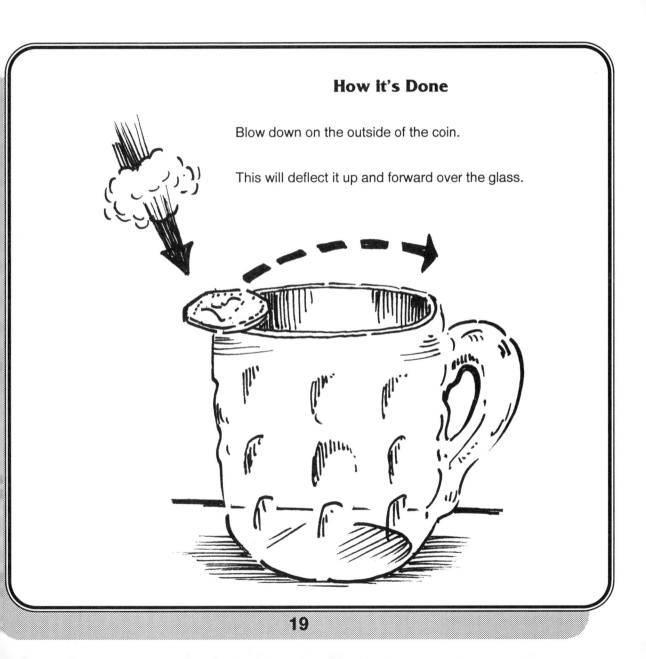

TRICKY BOTTLE TOP

This trick needs quite a bit of practice before you challenge your friends

What You Need:
* Any 1/2 pint beer bottle
* A bottle top

The Set Up
Place the bottle top upside down next to the bottle.

The Challenge

Using your forefinger tip only, take the 'top' up the side of the bottle until it rests upside down on the top of the bottle.

Now, still only using your forefinger tip, turn the 'top' right way up, (still on top of bottle).

Now, still using only the tip of your forefinger, turn the top once more upside down (still on top of bottle)

Return the top to the base of the bottle.

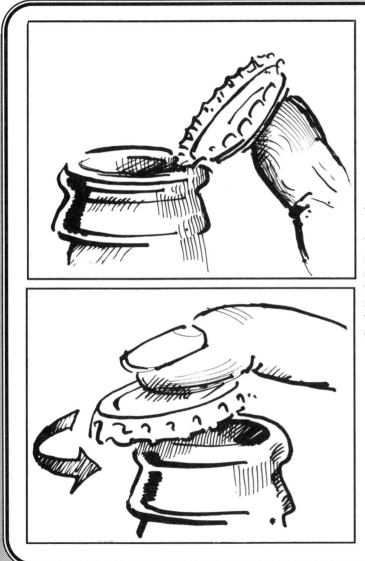

How it's Done

This is more skill than trick.

The secret is to 'roll' the top round the rim of the bottle on the second 'turn' sliding tip of the forefinger over the top at the same time, enabling the top to be flipped the right way up once more.

'Good luck!'

IRON THUMBS

Iron Thumbs is a great trick to do (if, like me, you're 5'7" and 10 stone soaking wet) on someone who is big and strong. They get very frustrated to think you may be stronger than them!

What You Need:

* An empty beer bottle

The Set Up
Place the bottle on its side on the edge of a bar or table.

The Challenge
Using only your two thumbs holding the bottle at the end of the neck, raise the bottle into the air horizontally.

The Failure
Your friend will attempt this only to find the bottle is far too heavy to lift horizontally and the base of the bottle will stay on the bar or table.

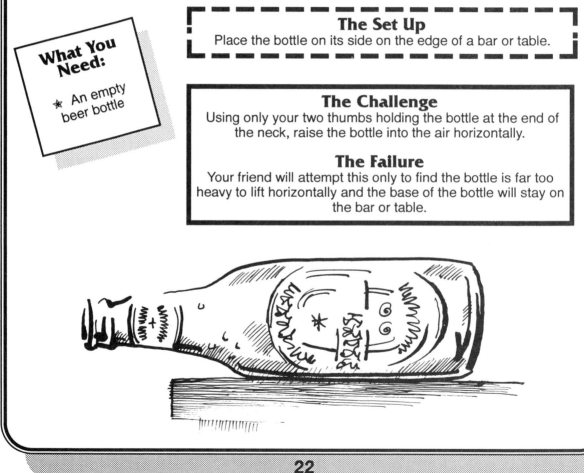

How it's Done

Linking the fingers of both hands with thumbs pointing away from you, approach the bottle 'end on'. Now angle your thumbs downwards at 45 degrees between the two moulded lips on the end of the neck.

This will enable you to use your thumbs as levers.

Apply pressure and raise the bottle.

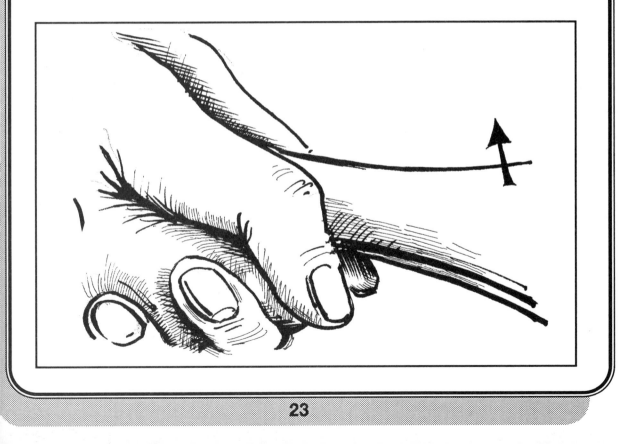

OVER THE WIBBLY WOBBLY WAY

This is a trick we first saw whilst on a skiing holiday. We thought the trick was great but couldn't think of a suitable title for it ... until, that is, Ian saw me hurtling down the side of the mountain completely out of control! This title came to him in a flash!

What You Need:
* ⚹ An olive or glacé cherry
* ⚹ A brandy glass
* ⚹ Three whisky tumblers
* ⚹ A straw

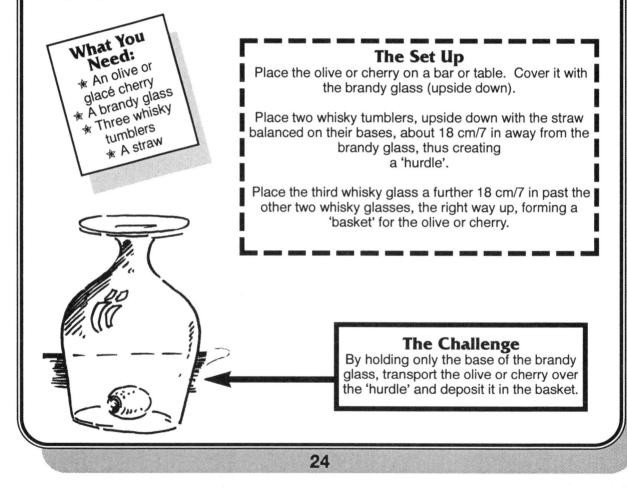

The Set Up
Place the olive or cherry on a bar or table. Cover it with the brandy glass (upside down).

Place two whisky tumblers, upside down with the straw balanced on their bases, about 18 cm/7 in away from the brandy glass, thus creating a 'hurdle'.

Place the third whisky glass a further 18 cm/7 in past the other two whisky glasses, the right way up, forming a 'basket' for the olive or cherry.

The Challenge
By holding only the base of the brandy glass, transport the olive or cherry over the 'hurdle' and deposit it in the basket.

How it's Done

This is a very clever trick and not at all difficult with practice.

Holding the base of the brandy glass, start whirling the glass to create a centrifugal effect. The olive will rise in the glass and spin round and round. Whilst maintaining this motion, carefully move over the 'hurdle' and above the 'basket'

When you stop whirling the olive or cherry will drop into the basket.

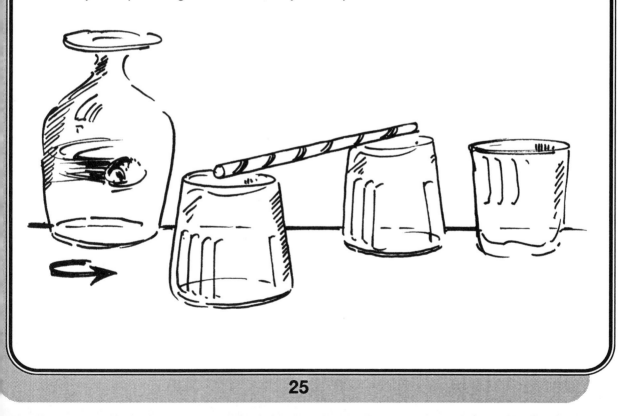

THE PAPER PROPELLER

This can be a trick or a party game! If you are doing it as a trick, prepare your cigarette paper in secret, and give everyone else normal papers. If you want to make it a game, get everyone to prepare the papers and away you go.

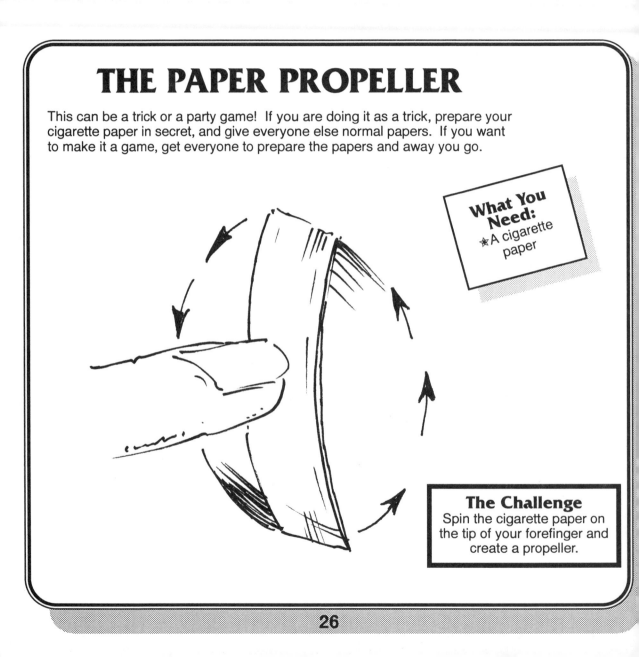

The Challenge
Spin the cigarette paper on the tip of your forefinger and create a propeller.

How it's Done

This trick involves a small amount of origami and plenty of space.

Take the cigarette paper and fold it in along all sides, about 4 mm/1/4 inch.

Open the folds half way back, thus creating a 45 degree lip all round the cigarette paper.

Now holding the paper between the forefinger and thumb at arm's length, start to turn on the spot. Your arm, hand, forefinger and thumb are now all rushing through the air in a circular motion. Release the thumb and forefinger holding the cigarette paper and point the finger in the direction of motion. The paper will start to spin.

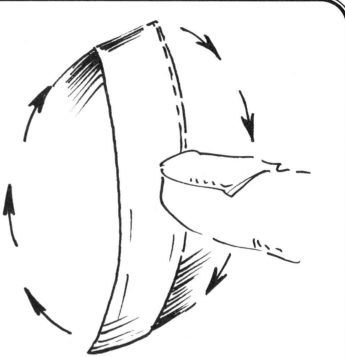

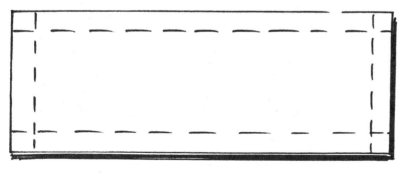

GLASS HANDCUFFS

Trap your friends very neatly with this simple trick.

What You Need:
★ Two large glasses full of liquid

The Challenge
Balance two glasses on the backs of your hands

The Set Up
Get your friend to place both hands, palms down, on a bar or table. Then balance a full glass on the back of each hand. They, of course, will be able to balance the glasses.

The Sting

Now, just walk away and they are 'handcuffed' to the bar until you return.

OLYMPIC DISCUS

This one is best performed outside. The more room you have the better.

The Challenge
Bet your friend you can throw a bottle top twice as far as they can ...
and they get the choice of bottle tops!

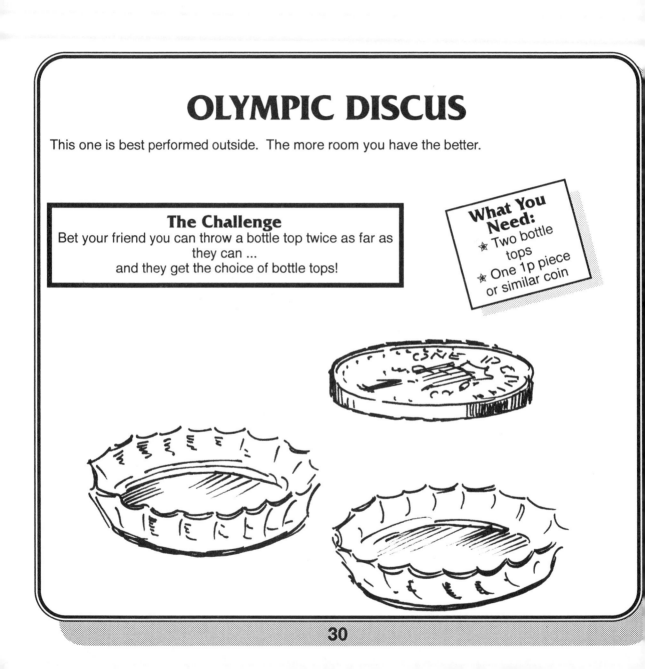

How it's Done

Give your friend an ordinary bottle top and let them throw first.

Secretly beforehand, or better still while they are throwing and everyone is watching them, hide a coin inside your bottle top by bending the edge over slightly. This gives extra weight and the top will travel much further.

Simple!

MAGNETIC MATCHES

There are lots of ways to perform this trick! You can perform it on your own as shown below, or give someone else an ordinary matchbox and tell them to do everything you do.

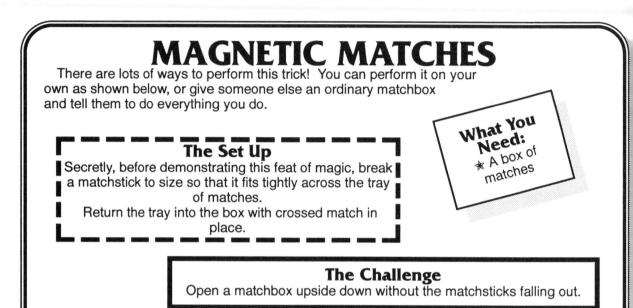

The Set Up

Secretly, before demonstrating this feat of magic, break a matchstick to size so that it fits tightly across the tray of matches.
Return the tray into the box with crossed match in place.

What You Need:
❋ A box of matches

The Challenge
Open a matchbox upside down without the matchsticks falling out.

How It's Done

Show your friend the closed matchbox and shake the box gently to prove the matches are inside, (they will rattle underneath the crossed match).

Holding the box the right way up, open it partially, just enough to be able to see the matches but not enough to see the crossed match. Rattle them gently again to prove the matches are not stuck. Close the matchbox.

Slowly and deliberately hold the matchbox ends between both hands and turn the matchbox upside down. Very slowly (adding drama) push the tray partially out of the box, upside down. Hold the tray between the forefinger and thumb of one hand and the opposite end of the box with the other hand.

Slowly pull the tray completely out of the box (the crossed match will hold all the matches, thus preventing them from falling out). Hold for a few second then gently return the tray into the box.

Once closed, turn the box up the right way and shake it to prove the matches are still there. Open the box and show the matches. Throw away the crossed match as soon as possible in case the audience wishes to inspect the box.

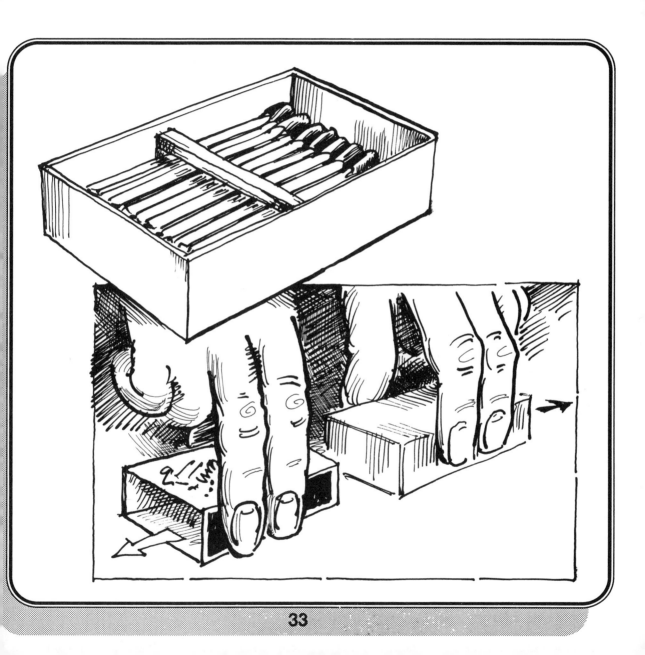

EGGSHELL AND KNIFE

Great fun at a party this; it will drive everyone nuts. They will all want to try it.

The Challenge
Hit the butt of the knife on a table or bar and make the knife pierce the eggshell.

The Set Up
Hold a table knife vertically above a bar or table, and place the eggshell on top.

How it's Done

Hold the knife loosely in between your fingers and allow it to drop with its own weight on to the bar or table.

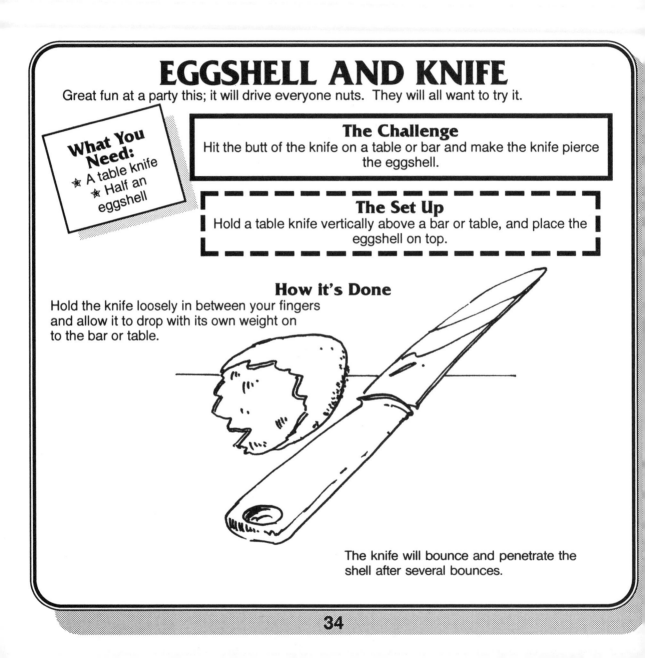

The knife will bounce and penetrate the shell after several bounces.

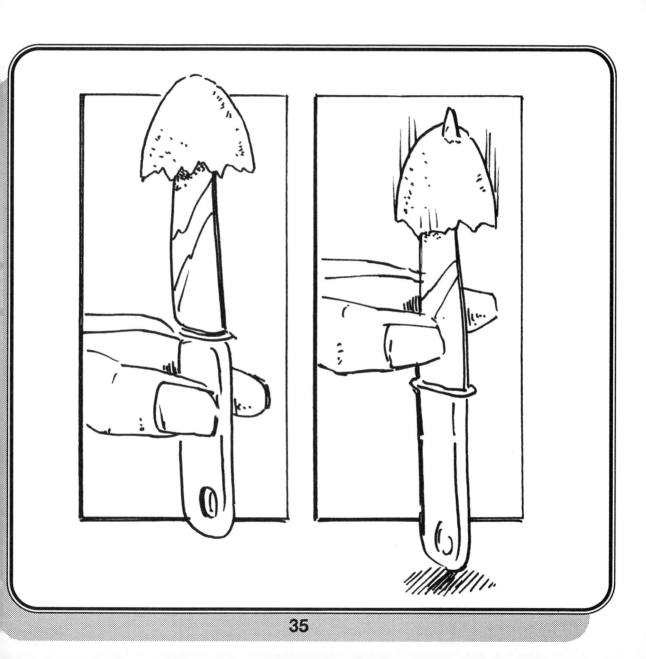

CHAMPAGNE CHEEK

Maybe I shouldn't admit to this in public, but I have won so many bottles of Champagne with this trick, I could almost be called a Champagne Charlatan. Since you need a Champagne bottle for the trick, the best idea is to let someone else buy it and then help them to empty it.

What You Need:
✳ An empty Champagne bottle

The Challenge
Holding the empty Champagne bottle, ask your audience, "How do you drink another glass of Champagne from the empty bottle?"

How it's Done

Hold the bottle upside down, then, from a glass full of Champagne, pour it into the indentation in the bottom of the bottle.
Then, just drink the Champagne! Cheers!

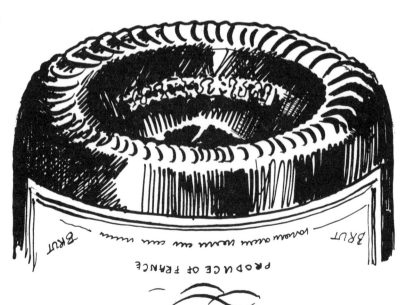

HIDE AND SEEK COINS

I'm sure we all know someone who likes to think they can work out how tricks are done! Well, this is a challenge you can let them ponder for hours - so simple, so clever. When you do eventually show how it's done, there will great shouts of AAHHRGHH! But only if you have done enough practice!

The Set Up

Decide on two points about 35 cm/14 in apart on the bar or table. At the point furthest away, place an upturned glass then behind the glass lean a coin so it is hidden from the direction of vision.

Now draw an imaginary circle (or with your finger and water) and place the other coin in the circle.

The Challenge

Without touching the glass, knock the coin (hidden behind the glass) over using the coin in the circle. The coin in the circle may only be touched within the circle.
This appears impossible.

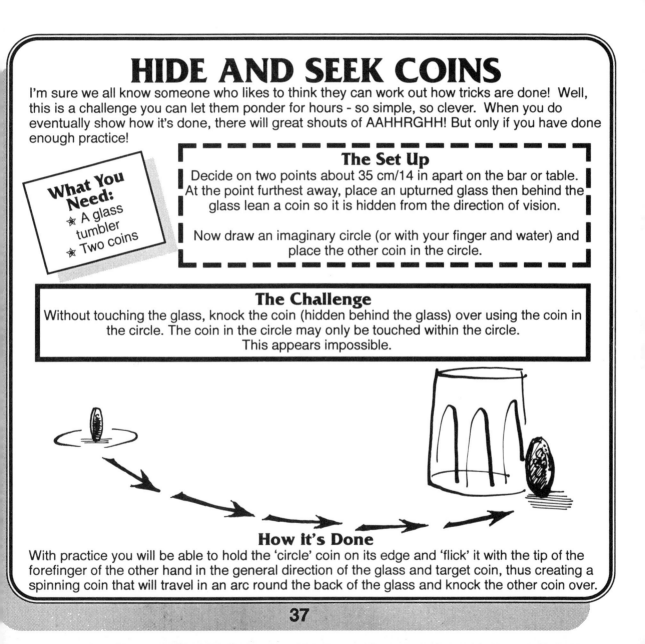

How It's Done

With practice you will be able to hold the 'circle' coin on its edge and 'flick' it with the tip of the forefinger of the other hand in the general direction of the glass and target coin, thus creating a spinning coin that will travel in an arc round the back of the glass and knock the other coin over.

MOVIE MADNESS

This is a fun trick only to be done with friends

The Challenge
Find the title of three famous films on the note.

How it's Done
After your friend has tried and failed, take back the £10 note and let them see both sides as you give them the solution.

You say, 'The three films are Elizabeth R, Jack the Ripper and Gone with the Wind.

But as you say Jack the Ripper, you tear the note in half and as you say, Gone with the Wind you throw the two halves over your shoulder, and RUN!

ASTONISHING ASH

NOT for the children this one, it carries a Government Health Warning. You will have to be a smoker to do this trick, which is more of a visual curiosity than a Betcha.

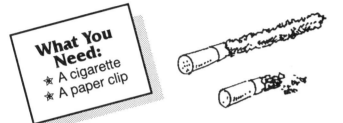

The Challenge
Smoke a cigarette without letting any of the ash drop off as it burns.

The Set Up
Remove a cigarette from your own packet, straighten the paper clip and insert it down the length of the cigarette (as close to the centre as possible) until the paperclip is out of sight.
Replace the cigarette in the packet, making sure you know which one it is.
Offer your friend a cigarette and make sure they do not take the special one.

How it's Done
You smoke the special cigarette.

No matter how much of the cigarette you smoke or how much you wave, not jerk, your hand about, the cigarette ash will not fall off. This astounds the audience especially if the trick is executed in a friend's home with a new carpet!

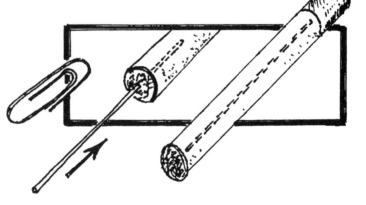

MYSTIC MATCHES

I wanted to include this trick in my first book for two reasons: it's simple to perform, but still very clever; and my Dad (whom I'm sure you all know) used to do this for the customers in his shop when I was very young.

The Set Up

Place a match vertically in between the end of the box and the tray. The match will now be stable. Place the coin on top of the box and balance another match between the coin and the first match. It is important that the heads of the two matches are touching at the top of the assembly.

The Challenge

Remove the coin without disturbing the match balanced on top of it.

How it's Done

Light the balanced match about half way along
its length. Use another box to strike the match
or you will dislodge the balanced matches.

The match will ignite and weld to the
vertical match and slowly begin to rise above
the coin, which can then easily be removed.

RISING DAMP

When you perform this trick I don't know whether your friends will think you are a good magician or a master of physics! Either way, it's very good and well worth doing.

The Set Up
Pour a small amount of water into a saucer. Place an upturned glass into the centre of the saucer.

The Challenge
Make all the water pass from the saucer into the glass.

How it's Done

Balance the bookmatch underneath the coin but pointing upwards (with top part dry) in the water in the centre of the saucer. light the match and quickly replace the glass over the top of the lit match and coin.

A vacuum will be created and the water will be sucked into glass.

A simple but VERY effective trick!

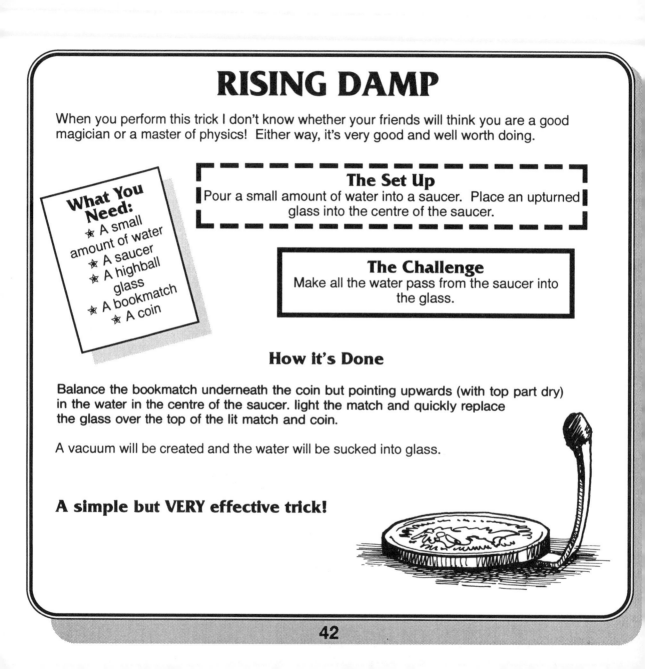

BOTTLE OF POP

How I perform Bottle of Pop depends on my audience! If I'm in a bar, I set up the challenge as follows, but if my audience is young children, great fun can come from telling them there is a genii in the bottle and that's what is pushing the coin up. Now, over to you ...

What You Need:
* A cold beer bottle
* A 1p piece

The Set Up
Stand a cold empty beer bottle on a bar or table. Making sure the lip of the bottle is wet, place a 1p piece flatly on the rim of the bottle.

The Challenge
Make the coin pop up at least three times without moving the bottle or touching or blowing the coin.

How it's Done

With warm hands, grip the bottle tightly in a clasping fashion and wait.

The temperature of your hands will warm the bottle, thus expanding the air inside the bottle.

This effect will eventually make the coin flip up at least three times, sometimes more, depending on how cold the bottle is to start with.

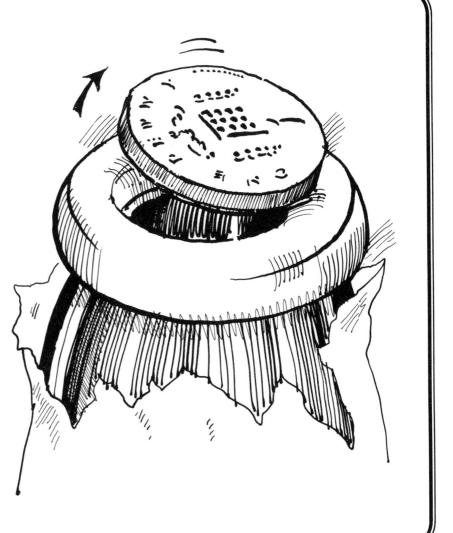

A LOAD OF BOWLS

If you have a physics teacher in your audience choose a different trick as they may guess this one!

What You Need:
* Four olives or cherries
* A soup bowl or similar dish

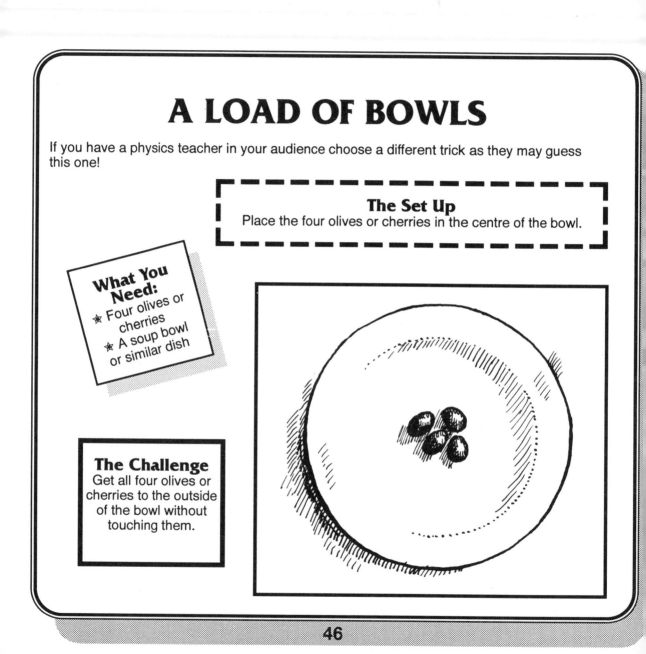

The Challenge
Get all four olives or cherries to the outside of the bowl without touching them.

How it's Done

Rotate the plate and all four olives or cherries will be thrown to the outside of the dish through centrifugal force.

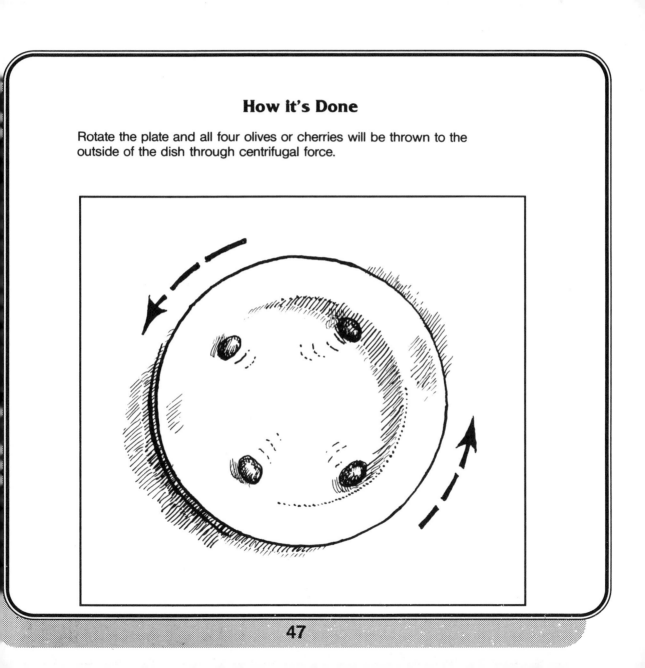

SILLY CIGS

The best part about this trick is that you do not have to be a smoker. You can use any packet of cigarettes that is lying around ...

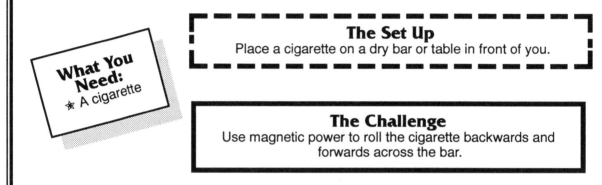

The Set Up
Place a cigarette on a dry bar or table in front of you.

The Challenge
Use magnetic power to roll the cigarette backwards and forwards across the bar.

How it's Done

Rub your finger briskly on your jacket or shirt sleeve and then point it at the cigarette. When your finger is about 10 cm/4 in away from the cigarette, discreetly blow at the cigarette and it will roll away from you. It is very important that nobody knows that you are blowing. It's actually more of a controlled breath with the lips slightly parted.

To confuse your friends more, rub your thumb on the bar on the far side of the cigarette, and make it roll back towards you.

Of course, when other people try rubbing the bar nothing happens. Only you have the power! To do this place your forearm flat on the bar the far side of the cigarette and by blowing down the inside of your forearm, as illustrated, the cigarette will travel towards you.

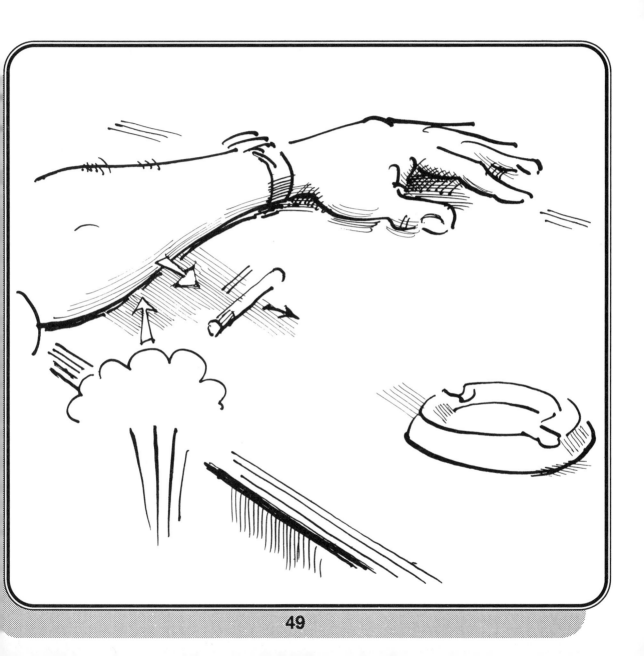

THE MYSTERY OF KNOTTY ASH

The Mystery of Knotty Ash is not how do you avoid paying your income tax! It's how to tie a knot in a cigarette without damaging it.

What You Need:
★ A cigarette

The Challenge
Tie a knot in a cigarette, without damaging it.

How it's Done

Take the cellophane from a cigarette packet and carefully open it out until you have a rectangle.

Wrap the cellophane tightly round a cigarette and twist the ends (like a toffee wrapper).

You will now be able to tie the ends together in a knot. Untie and remove the cellophane to show the cigarette undamaged.

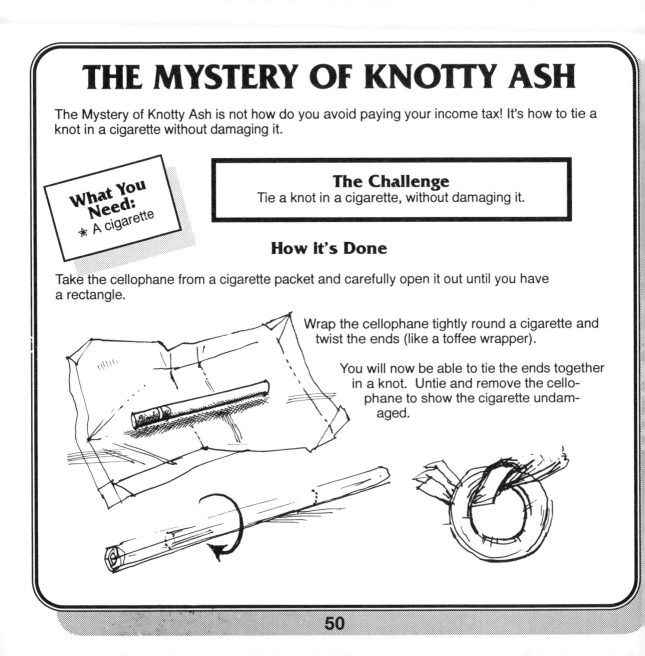

THE CIGARETTE LIGHTER

For this trick all you need is a friend with a sense of humour or, it's great to do if someone keeps asking you to do a trick and maybe that day you're not in the mood! Surely not!

The Challenge
Make a cigarette lighter.

How it's Done

Take the cigarette and snap the end off! 'It is now lighter,' you cry!

Alternatively, remove a cigarette from your friend's packet. You have now made their pack a 'cigarette lighter'.

'T' TIME

Once you know the secret of and have performed 'T' Time, everyone will think you have great skill with your hands. Actually, it's quite easy, but SSHH, don't tell anyone.

What You Need:
☆ A matchbox

About
1cm / 2¹/₂ inches

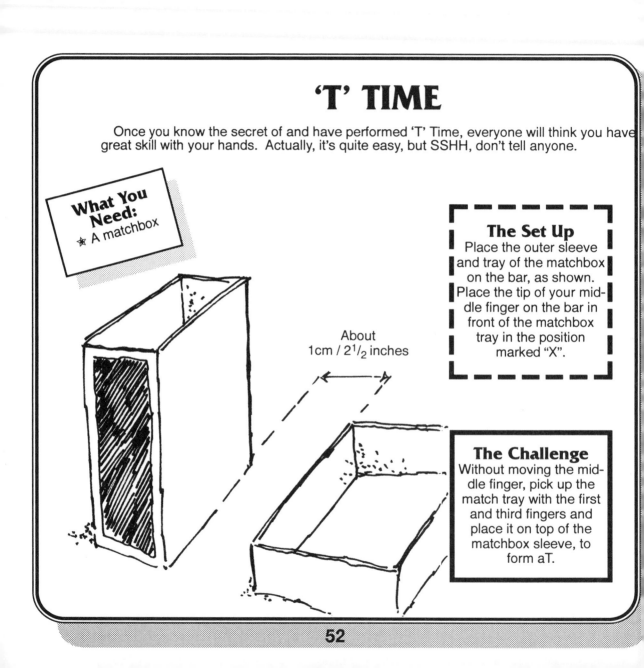

The Set Up
Place the outer sleeve and tray of the matchbox on the bar, as shown. Place the tip of your middle finger on the bar in front of the matchbox tray in the position marked "X".

The Challenge
Without moving the middle finger, pick up the match tray with the first and third fingers and place it on top of the matchbox sleeve, to form a T.

How it's Done

If you look carefully at the second picture, you will notice the first joint of the middle finger is bent backwards thus allowing sufficient reach with the first and third fingers to complete the challenge.

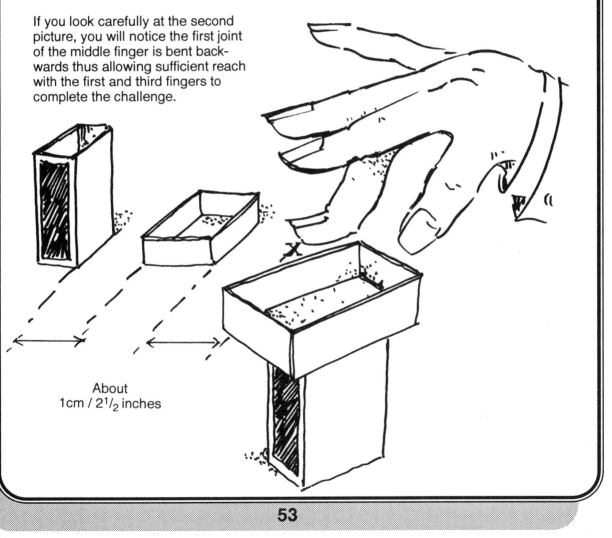

About
1cm / 2$^1/_2$ inches

DON'T BEER MUG

It's not what you say, it's the way you interpret it that's the key to this game.

The Challenge
Push the tumbler through the handle of the beer mug without touching the tumbler.

What You Need:
* A beer mug with a handle
* A tumbler
* A straw

How it's Done

Take the straw and put it through the handle of the beer mug and use it to push the tumbler.

You are now pushing the tumbler through the handle of a beer mug!

HOWZAT

This may not be cricket, but it might help you bowl a maiden over.

The Set Up
Place one glass loosely inside the other and lay them both on their side, with the open ends towards you on the edge of the bar.

The Challenge
Remove the inner glass without touching either glass.

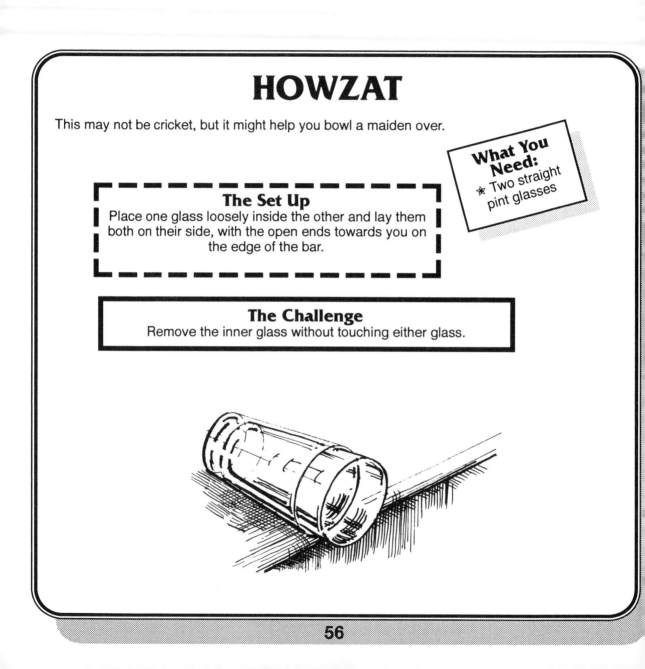

How it's Done

Blow hard into the gap between the two glasses.

The inner glass will shoot out into your waiting hands.

HOWZAT!

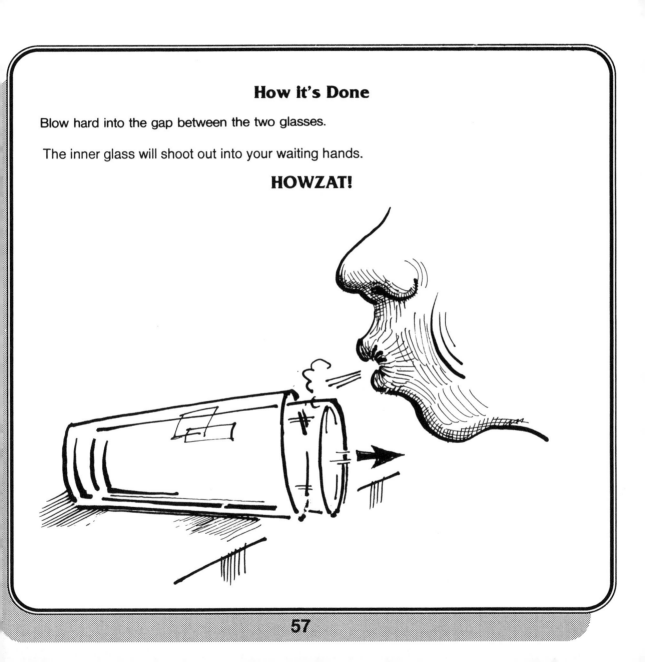

BLOW UP

I must confess that this is a trick that I like to perform, just because of how well it works! I hope you like it too.

What You Need:
* A large wine glass
* A beer mat
* A small coin
* A cigarette

The Set Up
Arrange the wine glass, beer mat, coin and cigarette as shown in the picture.

The Challenge
Get the coin into the glass without touching the coin, the cigarette or the beer mat.

How it's Done

Blow in an upward direction as shown by the arrow in the picture.

This blows the beer mat and the cigarette out of the way, leaving the heavier coin to drop into the glass.

PHENOMENAL PHORK PHEAT

This is a nice little after dinner trick, which, having performed it for friends many times, I still find hard to believe myself.

The Challenge
Balance the two forks on the matchstick on the edge of the glass or bottle.

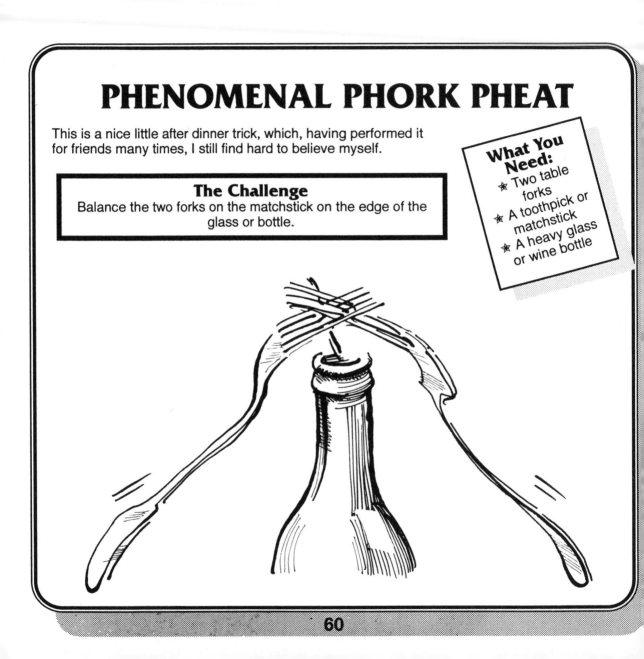

How it's Done

Place the prongs of the two forks together, one set of prongs on top of the other so they appear woven together.

Insert the toothpick or matchstick between the centre prongs.
The forks can now be balanced on the edge of the glass or wine bottle.

You will find minor adjustments will be necessary but the unbelievable effect created will delight both you and your friends.

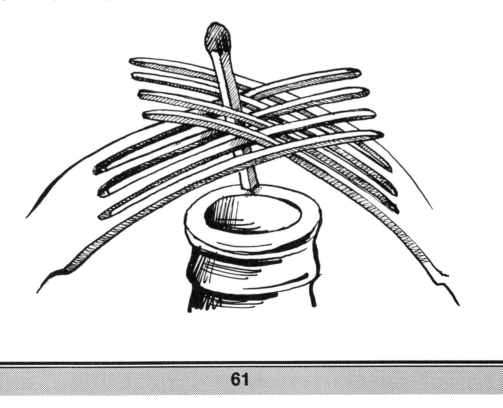

THE FICKLE FINGER OF FUN

A little sleight of hand is required for this one.

The Set Up
Stand a coin on its edge supported by the tip of one forefinger.

The Challenge
Make the coin spin away from your finger.

How it's done

With your other forefinger, stroke the length of the finger supporting the coin several times, giving the impression that you are creating a mystical force.

On the final stroke, clip the edge of the coin with your thumb - without, of course, anybody noticing. This will send the coin spinning away.

BANANA SPLIT

You can set this up before a party and just watch your guests' faces when you pick up the fruit from the bowl and peel a sliced banana!

The Challenge
Slice the banana without damaging the skin.

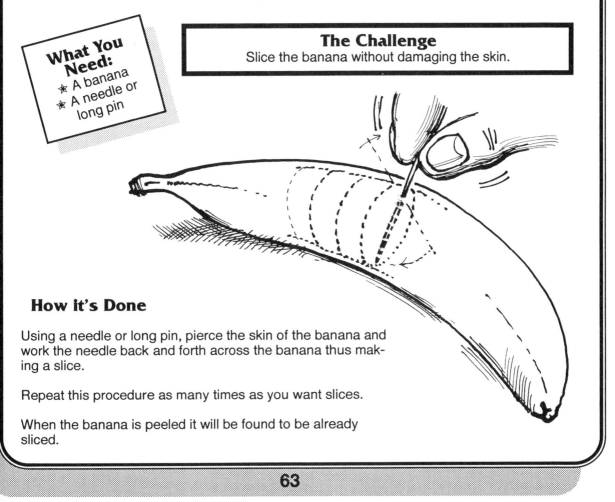

How it's Done

Using a needle or long pin, pierce the skin of the banana and work the needle back and forth across the banana thus making a slice.

Repeat this procedure as many times as you want slices.

When the banana is peeled it will be found to be already sliced.

BRIDGE OVER TROUBLED WATER

This is a trick I learnt in a very trendy nightspot in Beverly Hills, California. I was performing a trick at the bar when in walked Tom Cruise, who was there, he told me, researching for his film *Cocktail*. He liked my trick and introduced me to his friend Emileo Estevez, who showed me this trick you are about to learn. Emileo set the challenge and then I sat concentrating very hard trying to work it out. I was so caught up in the trick that I missed Madonna walking in, sitting down and saying, 'Hi Martin'. She wasn't put off by my lack of response, instead she blew softly in my ear, ran her fingers through my hair and kissed me passionately on the lips and suggested we do something I am not prepared to put into print. I ignored all of this and was able to work out how to do the trick.

Of course, all of this is a pack of lies, but it's better than telling the truth and saying I got this trick from a drunk in Scunthorpe.

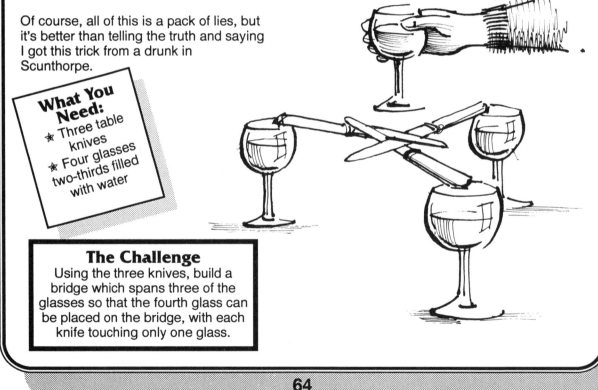

What You Need:
* Three table knives
* Four glasses two-thirds filled with water

The Challenge
Using the three knives, build a bridge which spans three of the glasses so that the fourth glass can be placed on the bridge, with each knife touching only one glass.

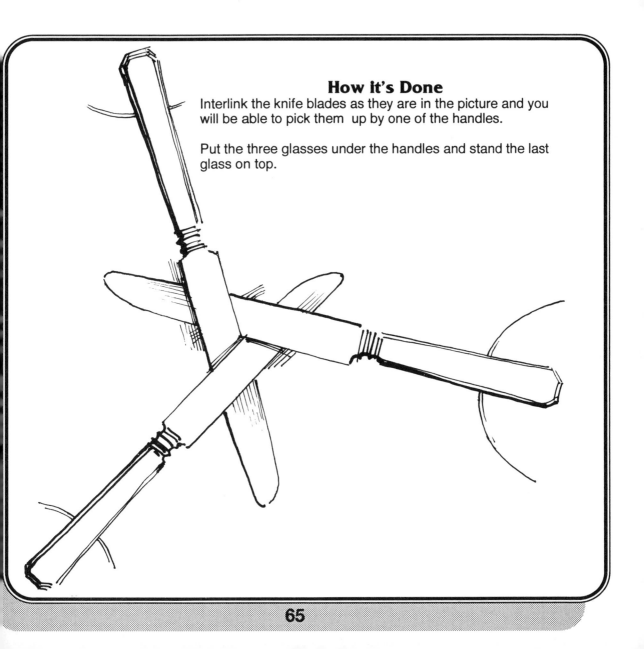

How it's Done

Interlink the knife blades as they are in the picture and you will be able to pick them up by one of the handles.

Put the three glasses under the handles and stand the last glass on top.

MARTIN'S MAGNIFICENT SEVEN

Here's something that can't fail to go down well - in more ways than one!

The Challenge
Pour seven liqueurs into one glass without them mixing together.

What You Need:
* White Anisette
* Creme de Cacao
* Créme de Menthe
* Apricot Liqueur
* Triple Sec
* Chartreuse
* Cognac

How it's Done

It is imperative that the liqueurs go into the glass in the order given (because each one has a different specific gravity which depends on the proportions of sugar, water and alcohol).

Line up the bottles with the heaviest liqueur first and the lightest, (which in this case is Cognac) at the end.

Pour a quantity of the heaviest liqueur, White Anisette into a thin liqueur glass.

Take a similar quantity of liqueur, the second heaviest and dribble it slowly from a spoon down the inside of the glass, so that it does not mix with the liqueur below but floats on it, spreading it into a layer of contrasting colour.

Repeat the process, being careful not to disturb the glass, until all seven liqueurs are neatly arranged in layers.

Once you have made Martin's Magnificent Seven there are three ways to enjoy drinking it!
1. Using a thin straw sipping one layer at a time, top to bottom.
2. Again using a thin straw sipping one layer at a time, bottom to top.
3. For the more discerning palate, aim it down your neck in one!

STRING 'EM ALONG

Do you have a wicked sense of humour? You do! Then read on ...

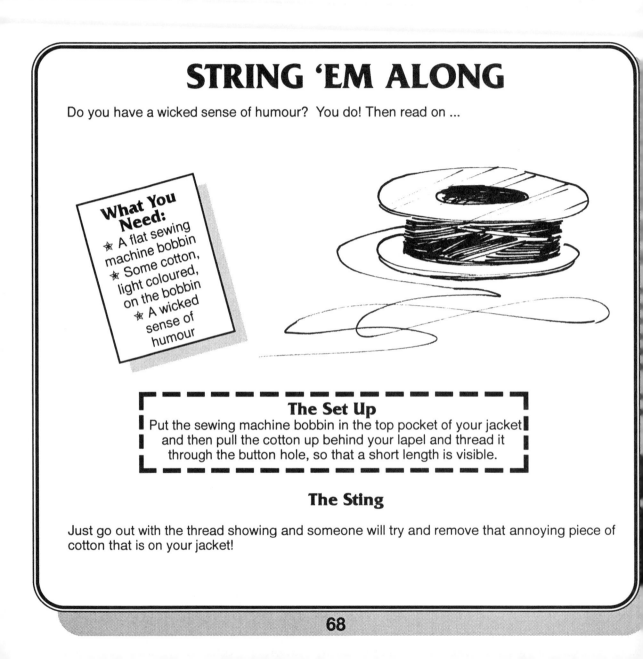

The Set Up
Put the sewing machine bobbin in the top pocket of your jacket and then pull the cotton up behind your lapel and thread it through the button hole, so that a short length is visible.

The Sting

Just go out with the thread showing and someone will try and remove that annoying piece of cotton that is on your jacket!

SLOW HAND FLUKE

This is a stunt for the show off that is in us all. Although it looks very skilful, it is actually very easy and can be performed after only a little practice.

What You Need:
* A coin
* A glass
* A snooker table
* A ball and cue

The Challenge
Hit a ball with your cue, strike a coin on the table then drive the coin into an upright glass.

How it's Done

OK, so it looks and reads difficult ... but try it!

Place the glass on the table's edge as shown and put your coin on the edge of the table, just in front of the glass. Strike a ball from across the table in a direct line toward the coin and glass, (some practice shots will tell you how hard to hit).

Correctly performed, the coin will flip up and fall into the glass.

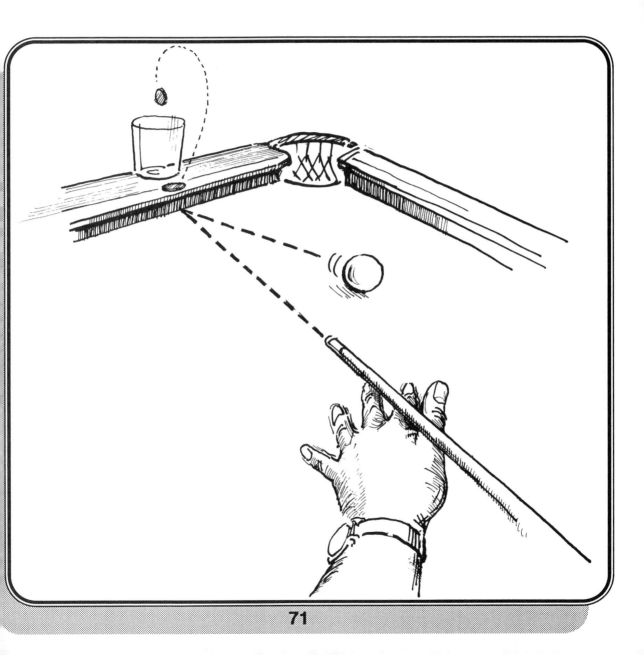

SLIME GENTLEMEN PLEASE

If you have a grumpy barman that you would like to get one over on, then this stunt is for you!

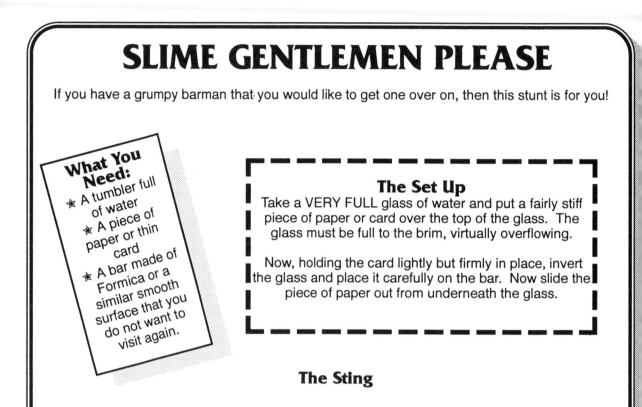

What You Need:
* A tumbler full of water
* A piece of paper or thin card
* A bar made of Formica or a similar smooth surface that you do not want to visit again.

The Set Up

Take a VERY FULL glass of water and put a fairly stiff piece of paper or card over the top of the glass. The glass must be full to the brim, virtually overflowing.

Now, holding the card lightly but firmly in place, invert the glass and place it carefully on the bar. Now slide the piece of paper out from underneath the glass.

The Sting

Quickly and quietly leave by the nearest exit because the barman is now faced with an impossible task - to remove the glass without the water going everywhere.

To add to the fun, if you drop a coin into the glass before you invert it, when the dirty deed is done and the inverted glass in on the bar, people's eyes will be drawn to the coin and therefore not notice the glass is full of water until it's too late.

TRICKY TRIANGLES

Simple but very effective!

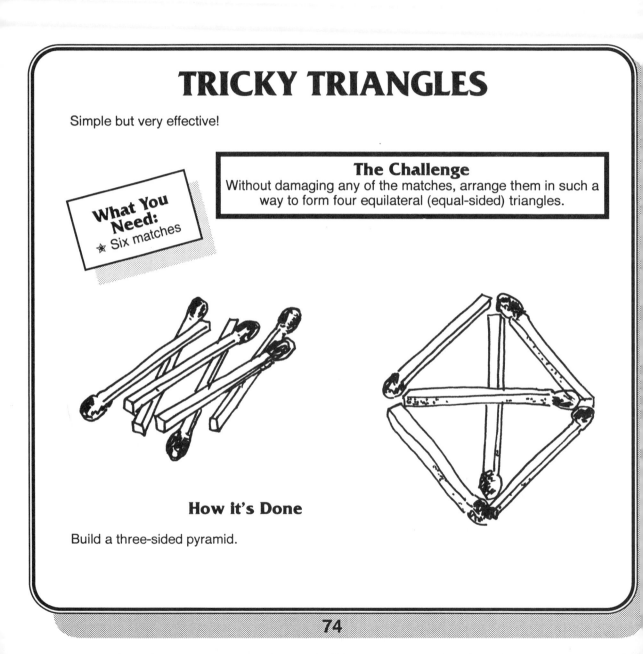

The Challenge
Without damaging any of the matches, arrange them in such a way to form four equilateral (equal-sided) triangles.

How it's Done

Build a three-sided pyramid.

DON'T BEER DRIP

This one is not so much a trick, it's more of a 'betcha'.

What You Need:
* A glass of beer

The Set Up
Drink the beer!

The Betcha
Bet your friends that no matter how many drips they can get out of the now empty beer glass, you will be able to get another ten.

How it's Done

After your friends have held the glass upside down and shaken as many drips as possible out of it, take the glass firmly in one hand and flick the open end of the glass towards a mirror or glass-top table.

You'll be amazed to see how many drips you can then count on the surface of the mirror or table top.

TABLOID TOWER

Tabloid Tower is great fun for a party, especially if you get half a dozen or so people trying it at the same time - have a camera handy.

The Challenge
Challenge a friend to balance a sheet of newspaper by it's corner on their nose.

The Failure

When they try to do it, the newspaper will flop all over their face, but not when you do it, and here's why.

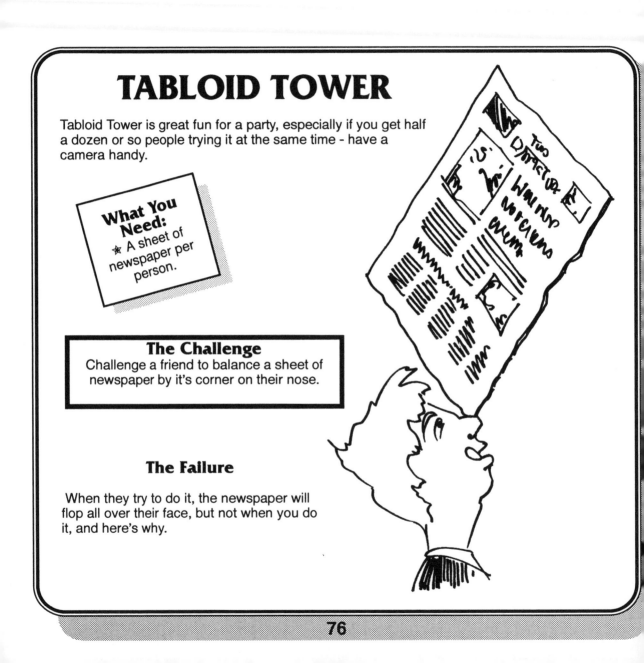

How it's Done

Take hold of the newspaper by diagonally
opposite corners and pull sharply.
At the same time, squeeze a small crease
into the corners.

This will now allow you to balance the
sheet of newspaper without it collapsing.

FIVE - COIN BRAIN TEASER

No trick with this one, just a brain teaser.

The Set Up
Place the five coins on the bar as follows:

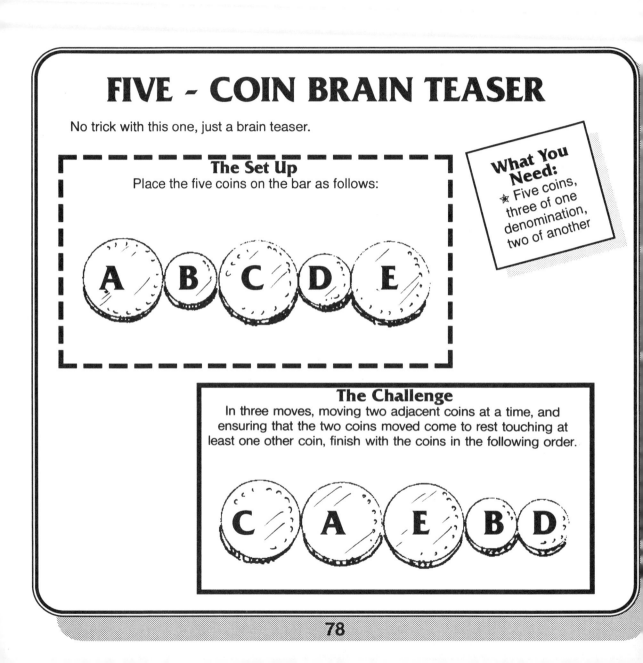

A B C D E

The Challenge
In three moves, moving two adjacent coins at a time, and ensuring that the two coins moved come to rest touching at least one other coin, finish with the coins in the following order.

C A E B D

How it's Done

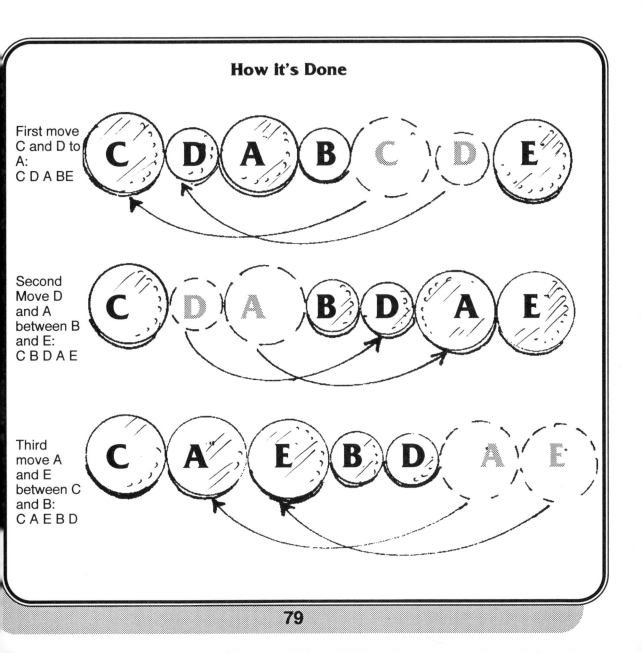

First move C and D to A:
C D A BE

Second Move D and A between B and E:
C B D A E

Third move A and E between C and B:
C A E B D

THE HAUNTED MATCHBOX

This is a very versatile trick: it's great to do for the kids and the opposite sex, by telling them the matchbox is a sexometer ...

The Effect

After you have placed the box flat on your hand, it stands up.

What You Need:

★ A matchbox

How it's Done

Open a wooden matchbox slightly and place it upside down on the back of your hand. Close the box, ensuring that a bit of flesh is pinched by the drawer as it closes. You may have to use a finger to hold the box flat whilst doing this.

Remove the restraining finger and at the same time close your hand into a fist. The box will instantly stand upright. When the fist is opened the box will lie down again.

With a little practice you will be able to make the box rise and fall slowly.

This trick can also be performed by opening and closing fingers, particularly little finger and thumb instead of making a fist.

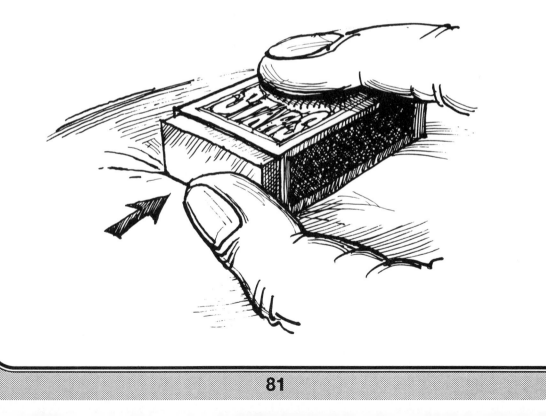

THE MAGIC CIRCLE

This is a classic - you can prove your infallibility time after time!

What You Need:
★ Six identical coins

Your Set Up
Place the coins on the bar in two rows of three as shown

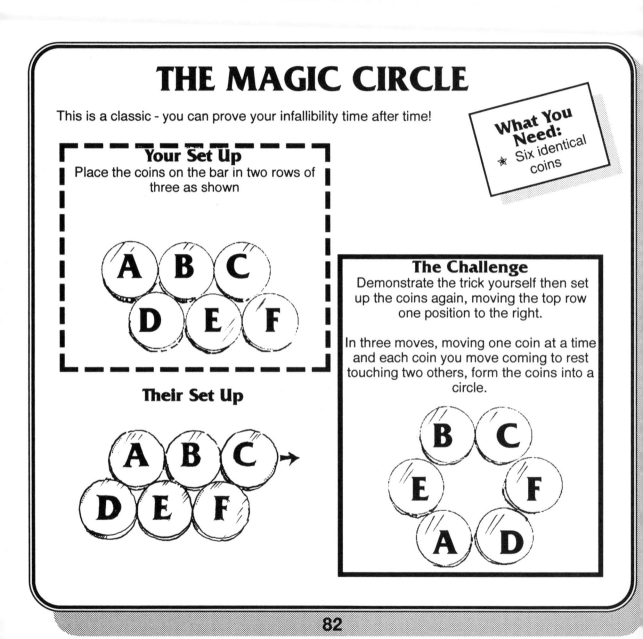

Their Set Up

The Challenge
Demonstrate the trick yourself then set up the coins again, moving the top row one position to the right.

In three moves, moving one coin at a time and each coin you move coming to rest touching two others, form the coins into a circle.

How it's Done

This is how you do the trick
First move D below E and F.

Second move E below A and B

Third move A between E and D

When your victim tries it, they will
remember which coin you moved
first but from their set-up they will
end up with a triangular shape.

From this, it is impossible to make a
circle in two further moves.

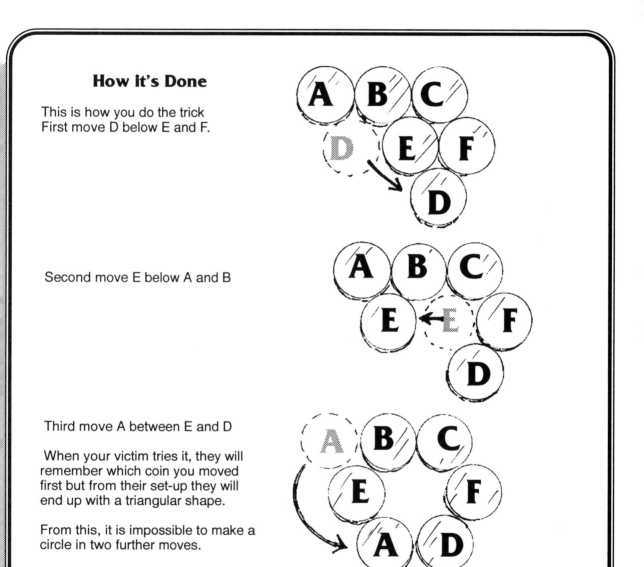

WHATA CORKA!

Whata Corka is a very baffling trick to perform in a bar or restaurant. One unique advantage this trick has over many others is that it can be repeated without anybody being any the wiser. So, this is something you could become famous for. No dinner party will be complete without you.

The Set Up
First, secrete the scarf about your person then mark the cork and bottle for later identification. Now push the cork all the way into the wine bottle.

What You Need:
* An empty wine bottle
* A silk scarf
* A wine cork

The Challenge
Remove the cork without breaking the bottle.

How it's Done

Tell your audience that you will remove the cork but because it is such an ancient secret you must do it behind closed doors.

When you are alone, take hold of the silk scarf by two diagonally opposite corners. Now work the centre loop of the scarf into the bottle. DO NOT let go of the corners of the scarf.

By holding the bottle horizontally you will now be able to joggle the cork onto the loop in the scarf. Now carefully and gently pull the scarf and cork into the neck of the bottle, and with a firm grip on the scarf, pull hard, and the cork will be drawn completely out of the bottle.

Put the scarf back in your pocket and with the cork in one hand and bottle in the other, return triumphantly.

VANISHING COIN

So easy, it's infuriating!

The Set Up
Place a 10p piece on the bar

The Challenge
Make the 10p piece invisible without touching it.

How it's Done

Put a pint of lager on top.
The coin is now invisible.

It will drive the barman mad; he will be sure he gave you your change!

HEADS I WIN, TAILS YOU LOSE

This is a con trick, based on the irresistible lure of 'Heads or Tails?' It is important that the bookmatch you use is a different colour or shade on either side - don't worry, nearly all of them are.

The Set Up
Drop a bookmatch onto a dry bar from about 20 cm/8 inches several times. Sometimes it will land light side up and sometimes dark side up.

The Betcha
Bet your friends three drinks to one that they cannot guess correctly which side it will land on next: light or dark.
On the next toss of the match you win all bets ... even if some of your friend have bet on one colour and some on the other!

The Sting

Once the bet has been accepted, start to make the throw but as you do so bend the match in the middle to an angle of about 90 degrees.

When it lands on the bar it will land on its edge, thus making your friends' bet a losing bet.

90°

TUMBLER TEASER

This is a trick which I have performed in many bars around the world and on television in BBC's Les Dennis Laughter Show. It is another trick that always works when you do it, but not when anyone else tries it. Will they never learn? Make sure you go first then sit back and watch their frustration at not being able to do it.

The Set Up

Place the three glasses in a line on the bar with the centre glass the right way up and the others upside down.

Demonstrate the trick then set up the glasses again with the centre glass upside down and the others the right way up.

Your set up

Their set up

What You Need:
* Three identical tumblers

The Challenge
By turning glasses two at a time (one with each hand), have all the glasses the right way up in three moves.

How it's Done

This is how you do the trick.

First move B and C.

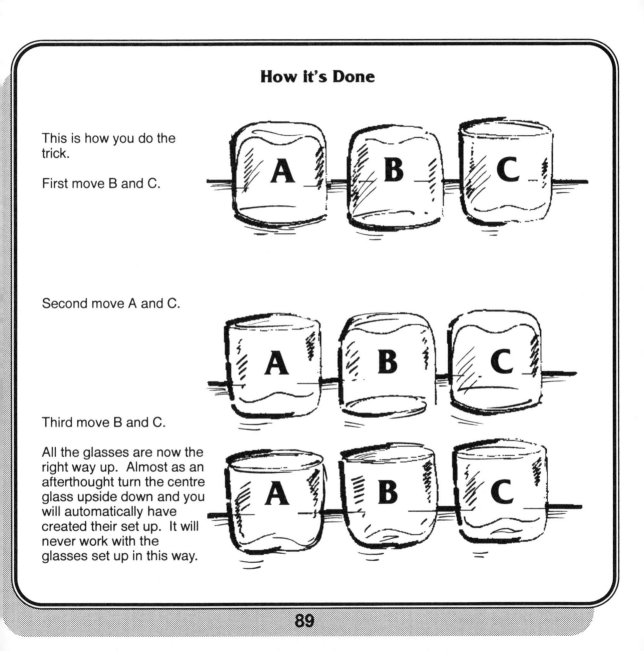

Second move A and C.

Third move B and C.

All the glasses are now the right way up. Almost as an afterthought turn the centre glass upside down and you will automatically have created their set up. It will never work with the glasses set up in this way.

CHEATS SOMETIMES PROSPER

This is a great trick to play on someone who likes to boast about their drinking prowess.

What You Need:
* Two pints of beer
* One glass of spirit

The Betcha
Bet your friend that you can drink both pints of beer before they can drink their one glass of spirit.

The only conditions being, you are allowed a one pint head start and neither of you may touch the other's glasses.

1.

2.

3.

The Sting

Drink your first pint and then place the now empty pint glass upside down over your friends spirit glass, thus making it impossible for your adversary to pick up his glass without touching yours.

Enjoy your well-earned drink.

PILES OF MONEY

No trick involved here - this is a bar betcha!

The Betcha

Ask your friend how many coins will they have to stack one on top of the other to make a pile the same height as a single coin standing on its edge.

You will be amazed to find just how far out your friends are. They will always guess fewer than the necessary amount. If you do not believe me then just look at the picture on the next page.

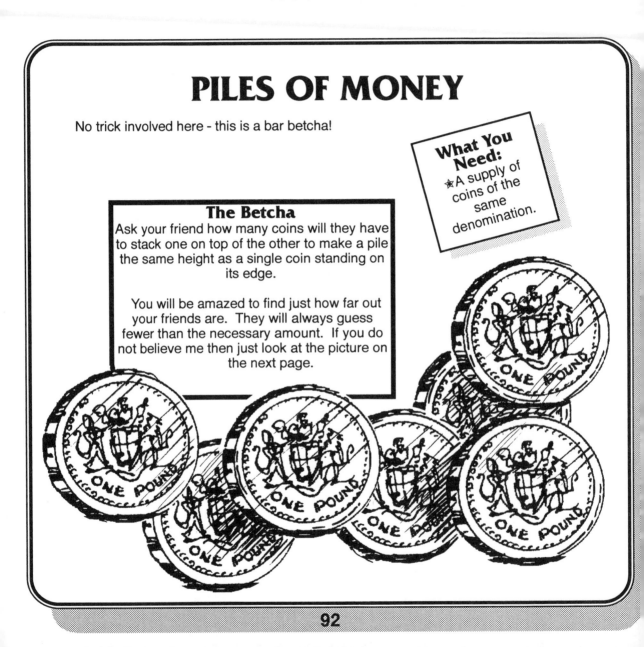

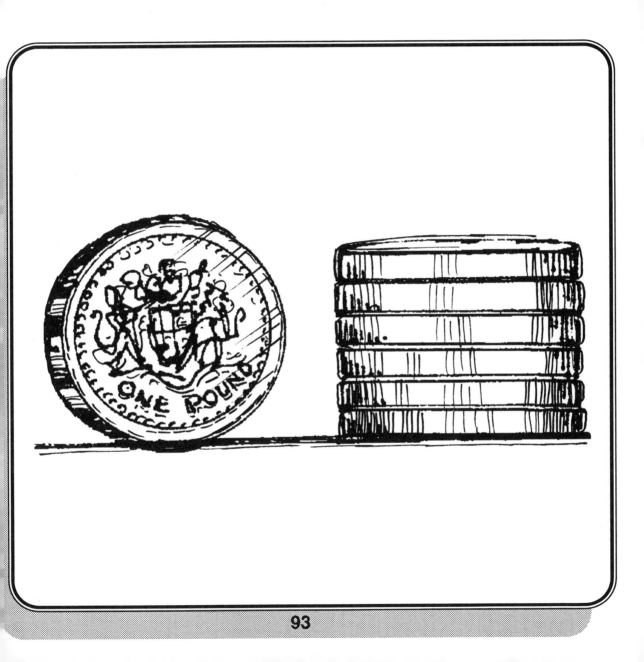

SHORT SHARP SHOVE

Short Sharp Shove is a very exciting stunt, and sure to attract a crowd!

Go on, show off, enjoy yourself.

What You Need:
* A pint of beer
* A matchbox or cigarette box

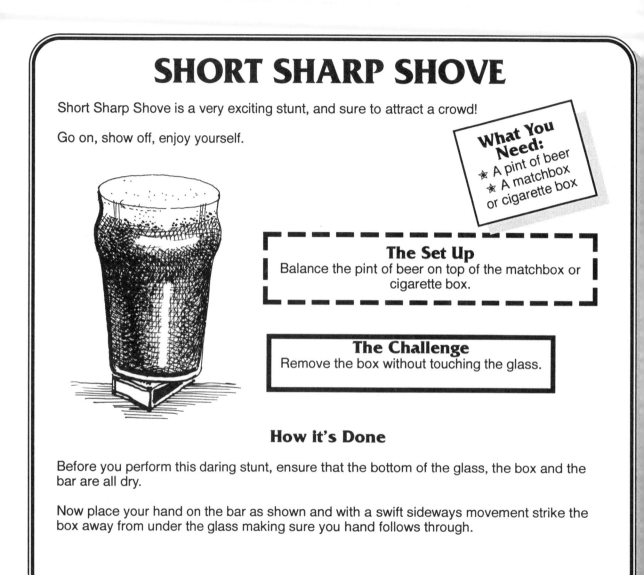

The Set Up
Balance the pint of beer on top of the matchbox or cigarette box.

The Challenge
Remove the box without touching the glass.

How it's Done

Before you perform this daring stunt, ensure that the bottom of the glass, the box and the bar are all dry.

Now place your hand on the bar as shown and with a swift sideways movement strike the box away from under the glass making sure you hand follows through.

The secret to this is confidence and speed.

BE BRAVE!